MU XIN

Toward Bravery
and
other poems

Translated by Mingyuan Hu

Hermits United
London · Paris

Published in Great Britain by Hermits United Ltd. 2022
First published in 2017 by Hermits United Ltd.
Reissued in 2022 in a bilingual format

The selection of poems, some hitherto unpublished, is made by the translator
from various Chinese sources
Original Chinese texts copyright © Mu Xin Foundation
English translation copyright © Mingyuan Hu 2017, 2022

Mingyuan Hu is hereby identified as the author of this work
The moral rights of the author have been asserted
All rights reserved
This edition © Hermits United Ltd. 2022
Fourth printing 2023
Printed in Europe

A catalogue record for this book is available from the British Library
ISBN 978-1-9998833-1-7

www.hermits-united.com

Mu Xin
Born Wuzhen 1927;
died Wuzhen 2011.

從前慢	10	Slowness Past	11
JJ	12	JJ	13
曠野一棵樹	14	Tree on a Moor	15
我紛紛的情慾	16	My Fluttering Lust	17
致 H. 海涅	18	To H. Heine	19
傑克遜高地	20	Jackson Heights	21
五島晚郵	22	Nocturnal Letters, New York	39
論魚子醬	56	On Caviar	57
號聲	58	The Bugle	59
《梵高在阿爾》觀後	60	After Seeing 'Van Gogh in Arles'	62
還值一個彌撒嗎	64	Still Worth a Mass?	66
甜刺蝟	68	A Sweet Hedgehog	69
十四年前一些夜	70	Some Night, Fourteen Years Ago	71
赴亞當斯閣前夕	72	Eve of Attending Adams Attic	74
卡夫卡的舊筆記	76	Old Notes of Kafka	77
五月窗	78	Window in May	79
我們也曾有過青春	80	We Had Youth	81
小鎮上的藝術家	82	Small-town Artist	84
如偈	86	Toward Bravery	87
詩人的額紋	88	Wrinkles of a Poet	89

Toward Bravery

如偈

從前慢

記得早先少年時
大家誠誠懇懇
說一句是一句

清早上火車站
長街黑暗無行人
賣豆漿的小店冒著熱氣

從前的日色變得慢
車, 馬, 郵件都慢
一生只夠愛一個人

從前的鎖也好看
鑰匙精美有樣子
你鎖了 人家就懂了

Slowness Past

I recall the days of my youth
People were sincere
What was meant was said; what was said, meant

Train station before dawn
Not a soul on the long dark street
A small milk shop steamed

In those days days were slow
Carriages, horses, mail, all slow
One life was enough to love one person

In those days a lock too was handsome
And a key, fine and shapely
You locked it; people understood

JJ

十五年前
陰涼的晨

恍恍惚惚
清晰的訣別

每夜, 夢中的你
夢中是你

與枕俱醒
覺得不是你

另一些人
扮演你入我夢中

哪有你, 你這樣好
哪有你這樣你

J J

Fifteen years ago
A chilly sunrise

In a daze
A lucid adieu

Each night, you in my dream
It is you in my dream

My pillow awakes, as do I
It was not you, I surmise

Others
Entered my dream in your guise

Yet not as you, not so good as you
Yet not like you, not so you

曠野一棵樹

漸老
漸如枯枝
晴空下
杈椏纖繁成暈
後面藍天
其實就是死
晴著
藍著
枯枝才清晰
遠望迷迷濛濛
灰而起紫暈
一棵
冬之樹
別的樹上有鳥巢
黃絲帶,斷線風箏
我
沒有

Tree on a Moor

Aging little by little
Withered more and more
Under a clear sky
Branches sundry and slight
The blue sky behind
Is death, in effect
Clear
Blue
So that withered branches appear exact
Bleary from afar
Grey with a purple tinge
A
Winter's tree
Other trees have birds' nests
Yellow ribbons, kites with broken strings
I —
None

我紛紛的情慾

尤其靜夜
我的情慾大
紛紛飄下
綴滿樹枝窗櫺
唇渦, 胸埠, 股壑
平原遠山, 路和路
都覆蓋著我的情慾
因為第二天
又紛紛飄下
更靜, 更大
我的情慾

My Fluttering Lust

Particularly on a night soundless
My lust is boundless
Falling fluttering down
Decking out tree branches, window lattices
Lip eddies, bosom jetties, hip valleys
Plains, mountains, path upon path
All blanketed under my lust
For the following day
Falling again fluttering down
Still more soundless, still more boundless
My lust

致 H. 海涅

恩是動蕩的
讎也在動蕩
愛情之船
滿甲板俊逌水手
從來沒有羅盤
沒有船長
一天無名的星象
哦, 當你執著羅盤
抬頭善觀星象
儼然是位英明船長
那時, 那時
你已不在愛情的船上

To H. Heine

Mercy wavers
Enmity wavers
A barque of love
A deck full of stunning sailors
Never a compass
Nor a captain
A sky full of nameless stars
O, as you, compass in hand
Look up, astrologically discerning
Solemn as a captain, and sage
Then, then
Off the Barque of Love you are, already

傑克遜高地

五月將盡
連日強光普照
一路一路樹蔭
呆滯到傍晚
紅胸鳥在電線上囀鳴
天色舒齊地暗下來
那是慢慢地,很慢
綠葉叢間的白屋
夕陽射亮玻璃
草坪濕透,還在灑
藍紫鳶尾花一味夢幻
都相約暗下,暗下
清晰,和藹,委婉
不知原諒什麼
誠覺世事盡可原諒

Jackson Heights

End of May
Mighty sunshine day after day
Street after street of shades of trees
Sluggish until dusk
Robins twitter on wires
Composed and placid, the sky darkens
Slowly, very slowly
A white house amidst the greens
Twilight irradiates windowpanes
The lawn drenched, sprinkling sustained
Violet-blue irises, waywardly luscious
All making a date to haze, to haze
Clear, benign, polite
Not knowing what to forgive
I feel in my heart — all can be forgiven

五島晚郵

十二月十九夜

我已累極
全忘了疲憊
我慳吝自守
一路佈施著回來
我憂心怔忡
對著燈微笑不止
我為肢體衰孱而惶惑
胸中瀰漫青春活力
你是亟待命名的神
你的臂已圍過我的頸
我望見新天新地了
猶在懸崖峭壁徘徊
雖然,我願以七船痛苦
換半茶匙幸樂
猛記起少年時熟誦的詩
詩中的童僧叫道
讓我嚐一滴蜜
我便死去

十二月廿八晚

每次珍重道再見
昨晚,我悄悄遁去
待你察覺我已走了
起一瞬永別之感
你會猜知我在後悔
你猜知了
我的後悔便終止
又無悔地向你行來

不成文的肌膚之親
太可能毀掉
你金字塔內的我
近月以還,憬明,迷茫
驟濃驟淡的悲喜交替
廢園中枇杷花藥性的甜香
嚴靜,夕陽之美
以及我愛你

明知站在深淵邊
一旦你擯我,棄我
也是福了的
不能愛,能思念
人被思念時
知或不知
已在思念者的懷裡
自踵至頂的你呵

安息日,小徑獨步
枯枝刺滿藍空
樹下一灘一灘殘雪
滋潤的寒風拂面
真願永生走下去
什麼也沒有
就只我愛你
傷翅而緩緩翔行

除夕·夜

本年的晴朗末日
從別處傳悉你的心意後
換了另一種坐立不安
飄墜般循階下樓
投身於晼晚的寒風中
路上杳無行人
黑樹幹後遙天明若鎏金
斜坡淡紅衰草離離
無葉的繁枝密成灰暈
鄰宅窗前飄懸紙燈
門檐下鐵椅白漆新髹
掌心煙斗鳥胸般的微溫
兩三松鼠逡巡覓食
遠街車馬隱隱馳騁
有你, 是你
都有你, 都是你
無處不在, 故你如神
無時或釋, 故你似死
神、死、愛原是這樣同體
我們終於然, 終於否
已正起錨航向永恆
待到其一死
另一猶生
生者便是死者的墓碑
唯神沒有墓碑
我們將合成沒有墓碑的神

一月三日

何謂紅塵歷劫倖存者之福
憶往事,悲慟淡如野墟炊煙
何謂離群獨歸驅車若飛者的喜樂
為你,我甘忍悽愴,滿懷熊熊希望
壯麗而蕭條的銅額大天使啊
也許我只是一場羅馬的春陰暴雨
還有幾次,多少次,如昏沉昨夜
我舉步維艱,沿城而行而泣而禱
先是你,絕世的美貌驚駭了我
使我不敢對你的容顏獻一頌辭
怕你怨我情之所鍾僅在悅目
崇敬你吐屬優雅動定矜貴風調清華
無奈每當驟見你的眉目鼻唇
我痴而醉,瘖而瞶,直向天堂沉淪

一月六日

你尚未出現時
我的生命平靜
軒昂闊步行走
動輒料事如神

如今惶亂,怯弱
像冰融的春水
一流就流向你
又不知你在何處

唯有你也
也齊了,懦了
向我粼粼涌來
嫵媚得毫無主意

我們才又平靜
雄辯而充滿遠見
恰如獵夫互換了弓馬
弓是神弓,馬是寶馬

一月十日

夢想的是
在你這裡，某夜
面對歌劇中聆到過的
百轉千回直透天庭的一顆心

靈魂像袋沉沉的金幣
勿停地掏出來交給情人
因為愛是無價寶
金幣再多也總嘆不夠

一月十二日

遇見你後
情慾的烏雲
消散殆盡
我對自己說
看這最後的愛
愛是罪
一種借以贖罪的罪
(拿撒勒人知道
且去做了)
噢拉比
我細小細小
只夠攜一個選民
拉比笑了,說
天國的門猶如針孔
兩個孩子騎著駱駝
也可雙雙穿過針孔
(那時的我
獨佔你瑰瑋的肉體
在駝峰之間
天國門口)

同前

你是真葡萄樹
我願是你的枝子
枝子不在樹身
自己無能結果

你是真葡萄樹
我將是你的枝子
結果甸甸累累
榮耀全歸於你

你是真葡萄樹
我已是你的枝子
枝子夜遭摧折
且明茁綻新枝

你是真葡萄樹
請你把不結果的
那些枝子剪去
使我結果更多

一月十六日

清俊的容顏
富麗的胴體
這次是你作勢引我抱你
明知一旁有人伏案假寐
我至今以為彼是你的倖臣
你張臂促成我上前緊摟偎熨
真沒料到我的情敵敗得那麼快
是第二度吻於你胸口
仍是那位置,更低了些
像歷盡風波的船
靠了玉岸瓊林的港岸
此番我不再憂慮冒犯了
知你喜悅我的頑劣
勿以我崇戀你的形姿為忤逆
我呀並非來自神話的蒼穹
我自紙質發黃的童話插圖中來
背上有橢圓透明的小翅的
那種笑盈盈的月夜飛行物
雅不慾進天堂入地獄
慣在草茵花叢間閃爍漫遊
做點好事,搗點蛋,無影無蹤
哈爾茨山的兄弟呀
他點巧如羚羊,彈琴而歌唱
我願吻你,你莫畏懼
吻後我便走,不會再來
是故你莫畏懼,讓我吻了這次
露西亞的兄弟呀
也不要世界的誇獎

在條條生命的田壟上
禾秸似的人轉瞬被刈光
夏天往往有這樣的情景
涅瓦河夜晚的晴空
異樣的幽輝異樣的沉靜
回憶起疇昔的幸福
雖已淡漠,卻又傷心
夏夜以它良善的清風
使我們默默遐想
恍如一囚徒
在亂夢中倏爾出獄
飄向草原森林
幻想就是這樣領著我們
重返青春年代的新鮮早晨
我愛你,不再離舍了
誠如脫籠的鷲鳥
掠入鬱鬱馨馨的森林
我誓作你忠烈的守護神
你雙目惺忪地喃喃
我應和,猶如谷底回聲
突然我轉身從樓梯盤旋而下
不見涅瓦河
也非良善的夏夜
街上寒風撲面
輝煌的櫥窗連成一片
玻璃和鏡面佈滿我的笑靨
首飾店燦若群星的陳列
何者宜作我婚禮的指環
聖母院神龕的燭光呵
為我證見遲來的滔滔洪福

十八日

低著頭款款款款走
不理誰個美誰個醜
腳下溶漾溫軟的雲
彳亍在雲的大漠上
路人再陋也不足嫌
再艷再媚也不足羨
款款款款低著頭走
猛省這是頹喪的步姿
人們見了會慨然想
一個淒涼無告的病漢
哪知我滿心洪福
款款獨行，才不致傾溢

廿一日

明天又明天
時而昂奮
時而消沉
明天又明天
回想往日平靜
如澄碧長空
把事業的五色風箏
奔跑著引高送遠
如今手執風箏的牽線
抬頭只見你的容儀
每當我稍萌怨懟
便越覺得你才是我的愛
你帶給我洶洶的生
我自心一再湧現死
渴望無遮礙之夜
畏懼狎習後的荒涼
你是聖杯旨醴
禁飲的誡令由我宣頒
今夕又訴以宏大計劃
你頻頻頷首雙目曄然
毫不知我為你燃燒
底層一片徹骨的冰
在死的冰上
起愛的火災
就因你已是實體而非幻影
才使我躓倒不能復起

一月廿六日

如拱門之半
我危弱欲傾
如拱門之另半
你危弱欲傾
兩半密合而成拱門
年華似水穿流
地震,海嘯
拱門屹立不動
眾人行過,瞻仰
勿知是兩個危弱之一體
離開我
你便倒塌
離開你
我猶獨存
哦,並非獨存
又有一半來與我密合
拱門下不復有年華穿流
是故你莫離開我
要知你的強梁在於我
皆因我的強梁在於你啊

二月十四日

愈近你
愈勿明你是誰
已是這樣近了
我退不回來
仆在寶藏門口
還得掙扎起身
自己殯殮自己

去國十載,歲月怡靜
遇見你,初初一驚
只是飄忽的身影
生澀微甘的目語
無損我宿葆的水木清華
詎料霎時雲蒸霞蔚
我如踉蹡中酒
鬱鬱沸沸不捨晝夜

披上海藍外套
八顆鈕上八隻錨
直立的錨無為而端麗
你自稱水手稱我船長
我願最後一個離船
或與船同沉海底
航向拜占庭,航向巴比倫
從來不靠陌生人的慈悲

除非我偽裝恬漠
握瑾懷瑜繁文縟節
御香繚繞間雍雍穆穆
由你詫異古國的王孫
狂放善辯忽焉守口如瓶
把滿綉祥麟威鳳的錦袍
揮手投之檀香烈火
青焰躍起杳無餘燼

分道時你說,永遠記得
記得什麼,都是虛空,捕風
你向西馳,我策騎往東
疲乏,焦渴,送葬歸途的心情
危樓蕭索,呆愕的燈
壁爐中濕柴嘶嘶如蛇鳴
脫落長靴跌倒在床上
周身冷汗無力再起

先知們最懼怕的胃痛催醒了我
灼熱的懷錶,凌晨四點
並非大難,熄滅愛,還復詳貞
你是春暉中阿爾卑斯山
我並非躍馬親征的帝君
這垂死的牧人,羊群盡散
猶在你蒼翠的麓坡吹笛
黎明,人影不見,笛聲永訣

週年祭

夜雨淒迷
壁爐火色正紅
記憶在
世事俱在
猶如多帆的三桅船
愛者(死別的, 生離的)
一一斜倚舷欄
回望, 無言
往日衣履
往日笑顏
夜雨中, 曳著音樂
徐徐向黑暗駛去

Nocturnal Letters, New York

19th December. Night

I am dead tired
And oblivious of my tiredness
I guard my integrity with prudence
And come home from delivering alms
Weighed down with worries
I face the lamp, a smile lingering on my lips
Bodily decline confounds me
Vernal force penetrates my chest
You are a god demanding to be named
Your arm having encircled my neck
Now I see a new land and sky
Hovering yet around the cliff
Though I would give seven ships of grief
For half a spoonful of beatitude
Learnt by heart in my youth, flitting to mind
A poem where a child monk cries
Let me taste a drop of honey
And I shall die

28th December. Evening

Always we took care to say goodbye
Last night, quietly I left
As you saw I was gone
And felt in your gut a farewell
You would guess my regret
As you guessed it
My regret ended
Again I come to you, *sans regret*

Physical intimacy, unwritten
Too inclined to ruin
Me in your pyramid
These few months, luminous, opaque
Alternating between woe and joy, now deep, now faint
A garden forsaken, wearing loquats' medicinal perfume
Severe, serene, the grace of sunset
And I love you

I stand knowingly in front of an abyss
Once you renounce me, abandon me
I will have been blessed nonetheless
If I cannot love, I can pine
He who is pined for
Knowingly or unknowingly
Is in the arms of he who pines
O you, from head to toe

Sunday, a lone walk on a lone path
Dry boughs thrust into a sky indigo
Scattered under trees, half-melted snow
Cheeks caressed by icy breeze
I want to walk on till the end of time
Nothing
Except I love you
Languidly I soar on wounded wings

New Year's Eve. Night

Last day of the year, sunlit and clear
From elsewhere I learnt of your affection
This set in motion another kind of agitation
Following the stairs down, as if floating, as if falling
I threw myself into the cold evening wind
No pedestrians on the street
Beyond the black tree trunk, a faraway sky bright as if gilt
Softly scarlet, sere grass dotted the slope
Leafless and dense, branchlets blurred into a dusty mist
From the neighbour's windows, paper lanterns dangled
On the porch, chairs newly whitened in paint
Pipe in hand, tenderly warm as a bird's breast
Looking for food, two or three squirrels patrolled
Horses, wagons, indistinct gallops from distant boulevards
You were there, it was you
You are everywhere, all is you
Nowhere are you not, so you resemble a god
Timeless and groundless, so you resemble death
Gods, death, and love are one since always
We end with Yes, we end with No
Unmoored we are, to infinity we sail
Till one of us dies
The other still alive
The living is the dead's tombstone
Only gods have no tombstones
We become a tombless god — you and I

3rd January

Talk about being robbed by life. Talk about survivor's fortune
Looking back, with composure I mourn, aloof as smoke on a ruin
Talk about the glee of a recluse. Talk about the elation of a lone wolf
For you I endure sorrow, my hope rising in flame
O, tall angel cast in bronze, august and austere
Perchance I am but a rainstorm in the spring of Rome
At times, time and again, in dimness, like last night
I lurch, I reel, circling the city, I weep, I pray
You. Your beauty stunned me
I dared not praise your poise
Lest you think my love solely for your looks
I marvel at your elegance, your stateliness, your finesse
At each glimpse of your brow, your eyes, your nose, your lips
Drunk I am, and dumb, and deaf. Into heaven I fall, head over heels

6th January

Before you came on the scene
I was serene
Walking imposingly in strides
Prophesying like a dream

Flurried I am now, and weak
Like ice melted in spring
I flow, I flow to you
But where, where are you

Only when you, you too
Are flurried, and weak
Flowing shimmeringly to me
Cluelessly charming

Are we again serene
Eloquent and clairvoyant
Like hunters having swapped horses and bows
Horses are magic horses. Bows are magic bows

10th January

I fancy facing
With you, one night
The penetrating heart
Once heard in an opera

My soul is a sack of gold
Handed to my lover *sans cesse*
Because love is priceless
My gold never suffices

12th January

Since we met
The black cloud of my lust
Has left
I say to myself
Regard, this last love
Love is a sin
A sin that atones sins
(The Nazarene knew it
And practised it)
O rabbi
I am tiny
I can take only one chosen people with me
Smiling, the rabbi says
The door to the kingdom of God is the eye of a needle
Two children riding a camel
Can both go through
(I was then
In possession of your sublime body
Between camel humps
At the door of the kingdom of God)

Ditto

You are the true vine
I wish to be your branch
If not in you
I cannot bear fruit

You are the true vine
I will be your branch
If I bear heavy fruit
Glory goes to you

You are the true vine
I am your branch
Ravaged overnight
In morn I sprout anew

You are the true vine
Cut off, please
Those barren branches
So I bear more fruit

16th January

Angelic visage
Lush physique
Your gesture led you into my embrace
As he, sitting there, pretended to sleep
I still think he was your favourite
You opened arms. I held you tight
My rival's defeat came surprisingly quickly
For the second time I kissed your chest
Same position, but lower
Like a weather-beaten ship
Against the jade shore of a forest
This time I worried not about offence
I knew you delighted in my naughtiness
You thought me not unruly to adore your shape
I came, in fact, from not myth's divine cosmos
But a yellowy-paged fairytale illustration
Oval, diaphanous wee wings on the back
A jolly flying object on a moonlit night
Wishing to enter neither heaven nor hell
Roaming twinklingly through the meadow
Doing some good, making some trouble, traceless
O, brother from the Harz
Deft as a gazelle, singing to the lute
I want to kiss you, fear not
I kiss you and I leave, and return not
So fear not, let me kiss you this once
O, brother from Russia
Uncaring of the world's cheer
From the ruts in the field of life
People as straw are cropped fast

A routine scenario in summer
A radiant dusk over the Neva
Peculiar light, peculiar quiet
I think of happiness gone by
Dejected albeit detached
Aestival night's kind breeze
Treats us to silent dreams
Like a prisoner
Freed in wanton reverie
We drift to the grassland
Thus fantasy leads us back
To the crisp dawn of youth
I love you. I will not leave you
Like a hawk out of cage
Swooping into wildwoods
I vow to be your guardian
You murmur, eyes dreamy
I murmur, echoes in the valley
I turn asudden and run down the stairs
No river Neva in sight
Not a kind summer's night
On the street, cold wind in my face
All around, splendid shop windows
Mirrors full of my dimples
Bijouteries with galaxies of stars
Which could be my wedding ring?
Candle light on the altar of Notre Dame
Attesting my belated beatitude

18th

Head down, I walk regally
Who cares who's pretty who's not
Velvety clouds ripple under my feet
I walk across a desert of clouds
Not loathing the ugliest passerby
Nor begrudging the most alluring

I walk regally, head down
It strikes me as a dismal bearing
Those who see me must sigh and say
A wretched sick man
They know not, my heart brims with beatitude
For it not to spill, I walk alone and regally

21st

Tomorrow after tomorrow
Now exuberant
Now despondent
Tomorrow after tomorrow
I recollect calm old days
As an immense blue sky
My career's vibrant kite
I ran and flew high
Now I hold the string
Looking up, all I see is your face
The more I tend toward complaint
The more I know you are the one
You bring me ferocious life
I am frequented by death
Desirous of an unhindered night
Fearful of post-intimacy bleakness
You are sweet wine in the Sangreal
I declare a strict ban to drink
Tonight I tell of grand plans
You nod, looking angry
Unaware that I burn for thee
At bottom, ice biting cold
Atop the ice of death
Love's big fire ablaze
Because you are real, not a phantom
I trip and fall, and stay on my knees

26th January

As half an arch
I am perilous
As the other half
You are perilous
Two halves join firmly
Time flows underneath
Earthquake or tsunami
Arch stands unscathed
People pass; admire us
A being of perilous halves
Leave me
You crumple
Leave you
I go on alone
O, but not alone
Another half joins me
Yet time flows no more
Hence, leave me not
I am your buttress
For you are mine

14th February

The closer I am to you
The less I know who you are
Now we are this close
I cannot retrace steps
Kneeling before treasure
Struggling to my feet
I encoffin myself

I left my country. Since, years of peace
I saw you. I was in awe
Only a fleeting silhouette
Eyes speaking words shy
Harmless to my preserved pureness
Forthwith, rosy clouds vaporise
I stumble and stagger like a barfly
Spleen boils and bubbles, day and night

Putting on my navy-blue coat
Eight buttons with eight anchors
Erect anchors, nonchalant and beauteous
You call yourself sailor and me captain
I would willingly be last to leave ship
Or sink with it to the bottom of sea
Sail to Byzantium, sail to Babylon
Never reliant on strangers' benevolence
Unless I feign indifference
Inwardly virtuous, needlessly courteous
Infinitely harmonious amid imperial incense
You gape: princely heir of archaic kingdom
Now flamboyantly glib, now tight-lipped

Satin robe embroidered with unicorn and phoenix
Flung into a sandalwood ocean of raging blaze
Green flames leap. No embers stay

When we parted you said, you always remember
Remember what. All in vain. Chasing wind
You gallop West. I gallop East
Done in. Bone dry. I come home from a burial
Shaky abode. Dumfounded lamp
Damp firewood hissing like a snake
Boots off, I collapse into bed
In cold sweat, unable to rise

I awake to a stomachache feared by prophets
Scorching hot pocketwatch. Four in the morning
It is no calamity. Quench love. Revive chastity
You are the Alps in the glow of spring
I am not a horse-riding king on expedition
This dying shepherd, his flock dispersed
Plays his flute still on your verdant hill
Daybreak. Shepherd not seen. Flute forever mute

Anniversary sacrifice

Dreary night rain
Beaming fireplace
Memories remain
All things remain
A full-rigged three-masted barque
Beloved (parted in death or in life)
Lean on the rail, one by one
Staring back, reticent
Erstwhile attires
Erstwhile smiles
In the night rain, trailing music
Sailing slowly into the dark

論魚子醬

禮物太精美
受禮者不配
千元美金
買十四盎司魚子醬
街頭喂鴿群

絕筆的心情
日日寫詩
再無什麼可悅
悅溫帶
而春而夏而秋而冬

何其壯麗的
最後的審判
最後會來,審判不來
何其寒愴的
沒有審判的最後

On Caviar

Overly exquisite present
Donee barely deserves it
I spend one thousand dollars
On fourteen ounces of caviar
To feed pigeons on the street

With every word as my last
I write poetry day after day
Nothing else pleases
Pleased with temperate climate
Spring summer autumn winter

What an exalted
Last Judgement
Last will come. Judgement no
What a busted
Last sans Judgement

號聲

夕陽西下
兵營的號聲

軍號不悲涼
每聞心起悲涼

童年,背書包
放學回家的路上

夕陽斜照兵營
一隻號吹著

二姐死後
家裡沒有人似的

老年,移民美國
電視中的夕陽,號聲

號聲仍然說
世上沒有人似的

The Bugle

The sun goes down
A bugle calls in a camp

Sad is not the bugle
Sad is my heart

A child with a backpack
After school, walking home

Sunset descending on a camp
A bugle called

After my sister died
No one seemed around

In old age, living in the US
I see on TV a sunset, a bugle

The bugle says
No one seems around

《梵高在阿爾》觀後

大都會博物館看罷
《梵高在阿爾》
下午四時
森丘帕克樹樹皆梵高
後面的天梵高天

小便急了
鑽進樹叢
SOS過後
又是一個心曠
神怡的男子

但見枯草地上
狼狗逐松鼠
松鼠沒命地爬上樹
上帝之德歷歷可指
(狼狗轉身追鴿子
鴿子撲翅飛起
上帝之德
真是歷歷可指)

狗在草地
松鼠在樹上
鴿子在空中
梵高在博物館裡
我在路上走

下午六時了
曼哈頓第五大道
聖誕節前三天的路啊
上帝之德真是左右歷歷可指

上帝
從早晨到此刻
我吃過一隻蛋一杯奶
你的雞的蛋
你的牛的奶
多麼快樂呀
就要下午七點鐘了
上帝之德無處不是歷歷可指

從銀行裡取出一些錢
夠買香腸和威士忌
下午八點鐘了
我在路上走
狼狗到哪裡去了呢
松鼠到哪裡去了呢
鴿子到哪裡去了呢
梵高在博物館裡
我在路上走

After Seeing 'Van Gogh in Arles'

I saw at the Metropolitan Museum of Art
'Van Gogh in Arles'
Four in the afternoon
Every tree in Central Park is a Van Gogh tree
Against a sky that is Van Gogh sky

Desperate for a pee
I dash into the shrubbery
After SOS
A breathtakingly
Delectable fellow again

On the grass I see
A hound chasing a squirrel
Squirrel climbs frantically up a tree
God's mercy is manifest
(The hound turns to chase a pigeon
Pigeon flaps wings and takes flight
God's mercy
Indeed is manifest)

The hound is on the grass
The squirrel is in the tree
The pigeon is in the sky
Van Gogh is in the museum
I walk on the street

Six in the afternoon
Fifth Avenue in Manhattan
Three days before Christmas
God's mercy is here and there manifest

God
From morning till now
I have had an egg and a glass of milk
Your hen's egg
Your cow's milk
Bliss
Nearing seven in the afternoon
God's mercy is everywhere manifest

I take some money out of the bank
Enough to buy sausage and whiskey
Eight in the afternoon
I walk on the street
Where has the hound gone
Where has the squirrel gone
Where has the pigeon gone
Van Gogh is in the museum
I walk on the street

還值一個彌撒嗎

我是世俗的
狼竄般脫越
笑語喧騰的修道院
挨在這裡,細雨
鴉雀無聲的凱旋門下
剔除煙斗的積垢
說老未老,說俊不俊
嘉年華如數告罄
巴黎現在也
窮得喜歡擺闊了
公社一百春秋祭
面對死者,生者只可素淨
旅遊氣,什麼都旅遊氣
艾菲爾的外孫買了尊小鐵塔
噫,這個巴黎
再憊賴,離十九世紀近
別處更遠更薄倖
從前的人,多認真
認真勾引,認真失身
峰迴路轉地頹廢
塞納河那邊,那扇窗
居斯達夫・福樓拜家的燈
即使亮到現在
這筆電費我也付得起

波蘭嬌客琴罷一瞥
手套帳單，馬車開銷
喉頭感到乾渴
開司米披巾確實奇貴
樣樣都弄得觸目驚心
上個世紀的人什麼都故意
自己真像渾然無知
巴黎精靈全靠這點神秘
人是神秘一點才有滋味
世俗如我，暗裡
明白得尚算早的
無奈事已闌珊
寶藏的門開著
可知寶已散盡

Still Worth a Mass?

I am worldly
I hop like a wolf
Over a laughter-filled monastery
Perching, in a mist of drizzle
Under silentious Arc de Triomphe
Cleaning my tobacco pipe
Not quite old, not exactly handsome
Carnival ran its course
Now even Paris is so poor
As to parade its wealth
Centenary of the Commune
Gazing the dead, the living duly proper
Touristy, all touristy
Eiffel's grandson buys a petit tower
Alas, Paris
So weary, yet so near the nineteenth century
Elsewhere is still more remote, more fickle
How earnest they were, people in the past
Earnestly they seduced; earnestly they lost chastity
Meanderingly decadent
Over the Seine, that window
The lamp chez Gustave Flaubert
Supposing it's lit still
I can afford the electricity bill
After playing the piano, glanced the dainty Pole
Cheques for gloves, expenses for the carriage
Onto the throat crept dryness
Costly were cashmere shawls

All was made to astonish
Everyman's manners were studied
They themselves appeared not to know it
Paris's genius is in this mystery
This little mystery, one needs it
Worldly as I, I in secret
Early understood
Things on the wane
Gate to treasure open
Treasure long extinct

甜刺蝟

你是船我是車
你是車時我是船
船和車要擠在一起
不是船裂便是車折
及至船載車車曳船
不外乎去修理去賣掉

初識你呀是個夜
樓梯轉角的一瞥
唇渦或眉梢
極微的某點特徵
我針刺似的感到
可能釀生什麼

瘋人院的鐵門口
用腳掃落葉
去年秋天誰知世上有你
喘不過氣來的瞬間
心中喝一聲懦夫
喘過來便軒昂而笑

好了
不再勞瘁於思念
雖然啊雖然
我是臨街櫥窗中的刺蝟
巧克力刺蝟
視之可怕 食之還不壞

A Sweet Hedgehog

You are a vessel. I am a voiture
When you are a voiture, I am a vessel
Were a vessel and a voiture to huddle
Either the vessel shatters or the voiture breaks
Before vessel totes voiture and voiture tows vessel
Winding up in a repair or a sale

We first met, one night
At the turn of a staircase, a glimpse
The corner of your lips or the arch of your brow
A minute detail
As if stabbed by needles, I felt
Something might be born

A madhouse. In front of its iron gate
Sweeping dead leaves with my feet
Who would have thought, last autumn, that you existed
For a second I gasp for air
Coward! Silently I yell
Catching my breath, with dignity I smile

Fine
I am not killing myself pining anymore
Although — although
Looking onto the street, in a shop window, I am a hedgehog
A chocolate hedgehog
Hideous to see, not bad to eat

十四年前一些夜

自己的毒汁毒不死自己
好難的終於呀
你的毒汁能毒死我
反之, 亦然
說了等於不說的話才是情話

白天走在純青的鋼索上
夜晚宴飲在
軟得不能再軟的床上
滿滿一床希臘神話
門外站著百匹木馬
那珍珠項鍊的水灰的線
英國師兄叫它永恆
證之, 亦然
乾了等於不乾的杯才是聖杯

太古, 就是一個人也沒有
靜得山崩地坼
今夜, 太古又來
思之, 亦然
靜了等於不靜的夜才是良夜

Some Night, Fourteen Years Ago

My poison cannot poison me
At last, not easy
Your poison can poison me
Reverse it, likewise
Only words said as if unsaid are lovers' words

By day I walk a steely tightrope
By night I feast
On a bed tremendously soft
A soft bedful of Greek myths
Wooden horses by the hundreds
Philosophical strands for poetic pearls
A writerly kin in England named it eternal
Test it, likewise
Only a bottomless bottoms up is the Holy Grail

Time immemorial is humanless
Quiet as tremors of the earth
Tonight comes time immemorial
Ponder it, likewise
Only a thunderingly quiet night is a good night

赴亞當斯閣前夕

一些異味的
細點子憂悒
撒落門口
雀兒啁啾,飛走
天色漸暗
憂悒在

年年名繮利鎖
偶值深宵
與少壯良友談
那類談不完的事
每次像要談完它
因而倦極
因而無力成寐

良友似一本
平放的書
架上諸書也睡著了
常常是此種
不期然而然的橄欖山

現在變得
凡稍有幸樂將臨的時日
便見一些細點子的憂悒
撒落門口牕口

現在變得
當別人相對調笑似戲
我枯坐一側
不生妒忌

現在變得
街頭,有誰擁抱我
意謂祝福我去
遠方的名城
接受朱門的鑰匙
我茫然不知回抱
風寒,街闊
人群熙攘

總之,龐貝冊為我的封地時
龐貝已是廢墟

Eve of Attending Adams Attic

Some peculiar-scented
Specks of melancholy
Shattered at the door
Sparrows sing, take wing
Sky evenly dims
Melancholy sits

Year after year, bridled by fame
On occasion, late into the night
I speak to a good young friend
About things unending
As if to end it each time
Ergo drained
Ergo too tired to sleep

Good friend is a book
Laid out flat
Shelved books, fast asleep
Often what presents itself
Is Mount Olivet unforeseen

It happens now
When serendipity impends
I see specks of melancholy
At my door and window

It happens now
When I see others coquet
I obtusely take a seat
I do not envy

It happens now
Someone hugs me in the street
Felicitating me on heading
For a lauded city far away
Accepting key to a ruby gate
I am lost, inept at hugging back
The wind cold, the street wide
A sea of people came and went

In brief, the day Pompeii is awarded me
Pompeii is already a wreck

卡夫卡的舊筆記

從清晨六點起
連續學習到傍晚
發覺我的左手
憐憫地握了握右手

黃昏時分
由於無聊
我三次走進浴室
洗洗這個洗洗那個

生在任何時代
我都是痛苦的
所以不要怪時代
也不要怪我

Old Notes of Kafka

From six in the morning
Studying incessantly till evening
I find my left hand
Clasping my right hand in empathy

In twilight
With ennui
I go thrice into the bathroom
Washing this, washing that

Born in any epoch
I would have been morose
So, do not reproach the epoch
Nor me

五月窗

五月窗,雨
濕黑的樹幹
新綠密葉
予亦整日濕黑
連朝無主地新綠
矜式於外表
心裡年輕得什麼似的
囚徒睡著了就自由
夜夢中個個都年輕
白髮,皺紋,步履遲緩
年輕時也以為一老就全老
而今知道,被我知道了
人身上有一樣是不老的
心,就只年輕時的那顆心

Window in May

Window in May. Rain
Tree trunks dark and dewy
Thick leaves new and green
All day long I too am dark and dewy
Day after day, pointlessly new and green
I may look mild and mellow
In truth I am fiercely young
Asleep, a prisoner is free
In dream, young is each and every
Wrinkles, white hair, listless gait
I too thought all would be old when old
But now I know, I come to know
The one thing that does not age
Heart, the heart when we were young

我們也曾有過青春

年輕時候，那光景
我們人生模仿藝術
不是藝術模仿人生
窗外二次大戰剛過
窗內十九世紀至尊

音樂是我的命
愛情是我的病
貝多汶是我的神
蕭邦是我的心
誰美貌，誰就是我的死靈魂

蘭心，法國小劇場氣氛
後排學生廉價票，請進
我們没有晚禮服、望遠鏡
照樣衣履光鮮，黑白分明
整個夜晚空氣一派康乃馨

我是小規模的博大精深
我們的流浪只限於路角街心
一天接連看四場電影
不要泰山、出水芙蓉
只看卡薩布蘭卡、血淚孤星

我們從不上下其手
十九歲不懂接吻
二十歲只敢印在眉心
好像神甫親教徒
將我愛你說成了阿門

We Had Youth

When we were young
Our life imitated art
Not vice versa
WWII had passed outside our window
Inside we revered the century past

Music was my élan vital
Love, my mal
Beethoven was my god
Chopin, my heart
Whoever was comely was my dead soul

Lyceum Theatre Shanghai, ambiance of France
Cheap rear seats for students, please come in
We had no evening dresses, nor binoculars
Soigné all the same, in black and white
All night long, carnations in the air

My erudition was small-scale
Our roving was around the block
In a single day, four movies
No Tarzan, no Bathing Beauty
Only Casablanca, and Great Expectations

Impeccable was our etiquette
At nineteen, we knew not how to kiss
At twenty, we pecked on the forehead
Like a priest kissing a believer
In lieu of 'I love you' we uttered 'Amen'

小鎮上的藝術家

國慶節下午
天氣晴正
上午遊行過了

黃浦江對岸
小鎮中學教師
二十四歲,什麼也不是

滿腔十九世紀
福樓拜為師
雷珈米爾夫人為友
我好比籠中鳥
沒有天空
可也沒有翅膀

看樣子是定局了
巴黎的盤子洗不成了
奮鬥、受苦,我也怕
先找個人愛愛吧
人是有的
馬馬虎虎不算數

夜來風吹牆角
艾格頓荒原
哈代,哈代呀

看樣子是就這樣下去了
平日裡什麼樂子也沒有
除非在街上吃碗餛飩

有時，人生真不如一行波特萊爾
有時，波特萊爾
真不如一碗餛飩

Small-town Artist

National Day, in the afternoon
Glorious weather
I have been to the morning parade

On the other side of Huangpu River
A small-town high school teacher
Aged twenty-four; undistinguished

Nineteenth-century at heart
Studying under Flaubert
Friends with Madame Récamier
I am a bird in a cage
Without sky
Without wings either

It looks as though I have settled forever
No more dishwashing in Paris
Struggling and suffering, I fear it too
For now, find a lover
Such a person exists
So-so; doesn't count

Night wind across the wall
Egdon Heath
Hardy, O Hardy

It looks as though this is it
Days are without joy
Except when I eat a bowl of dumplings on the street

Sometimes, life matters less than a line by Baudelaire
Sometimes, Baudelaire matters less
Than a bowl of dumplings

如偈

藝海如宦海
沉浮五十年
榮辱萬事過
貴賤一身兼
我亦飄零久
移樽美利堅
避秦重振筆
抖擻三百篇
問君胡能爾
向笑終無言
樓高清入骨
山遠淡失巔
人道天連水
我意水接天
肝膽忽相照
鐘鼎永傳衍
會當飲美酒
顧盼若神仙
被服紈與素
輻輳致而堅
窺戶多魑魅
幕重豈容見
晚晴風光好
大夢覺尤眠
每憶兒時景
蓮葉何田田

Toward Bravery

In art as in office
Up and down for fifty years
Eminence and disgrace
Now noble, now humble
For long I wandered
Traversing to the States
Taking cover, resuming my pen
Turning out books of odes
How do I do it?
I smile, wordless
High in my tower, pride in spine
A mountain distant, lost in mist
Sky meets water
Water touches sky
Loyal hearts in sympathy
Honour to eternity
Let us drink
With godlike abandon
Finely dressed
Journeying at ease
So much evil
Veiled from sight
On a day cloudless
Dreaming wide awake
I see my childhood again
Endless lotus, endless leaves

詩人的額紋

我寫著詩訣別故鄉
六十年後我寫著詩回來
比唐吉軻德少一分勇敢
比哈姆萊特多一份仁慈
朋友們,別哀憐我
小鳥在樹上叫得歡
只當我躺在床上不再起來

你們,你們都是好的
只不過沒有我好
我的好好在哪裡呢
好在我什麼都愛
我有富可敵十國百國的愛

Wrinkles of a Poet

Writing a poem I bade my home farewell
Sixty years later, writing a poem I return
Less lionhearted than Don Quixote
More tenderhearted than Hamlet
My friends, pity me not
A birdie trills in the tree
I am bedfast hereupon

You, you are all good
Only not so good as me
In what lies my goodness
In that I love all
I have love richer than a hundred kings